# The B
# Guide
# Men

Antony Mason

Oval Books

Published by Oval Books
335 Kennington Road
London SE11 4QE
United Kingdom

Telephone: +44 (0)20 7582 7123
Fax: +44 (0)20 7582 1022
E-mail: info@ovalbooks.com
Web site: www.ovalbooks.com

Published by Ravette Publishing 1998

Published by Oval Books 1999
Reprinted 2000,2003
New edition 2004, reprinted 2005
New edition 2006


Series Editor – Anne Tauté

Cover designers – Vicki Towers
Cover image: © Thinkstock
Printer – Cox & Wyman Ltd.
Producer – Oval Projects Ltd.

The Bluffer's® Guides series is based
on an original idea by Peter Wolfe.


The Bluffer's Guide®, The Bluffer's Guides®,
Bluffer's®, and Bluff Your Way®
are Registered Trademarks.

ISBN-13: 978-1-903096-95-6
ISBN-10: 1-903096-95-2

# CONTENTS

# THE KEY TO UNDERSTANDING WHAT MEN ARE ABOUT

What are men about? This is a question that has perplexed women since the first Neanderthal beefcake dragged a carcass into the cave with a hopeful grin all over his face. It is also the question that men ask today, struggling to wipe that same grin off their faces as they return from the supermarket minus several key items.

For five million years, science has been unable to answer the question. But where science fails, you, the bluffer, can succeed. A lofty ambition, you might suppose. But it is precisely because men have avoided analysis, that the smallest insight will instantly single you out as an expert. By absorbing what is contained in the following pages, and deploying it whenever the subject of men crops up in conversation (a far from rare event), you will gain the status of one who thoroughly understands the less fair sex.

A useful starting thesis is that men are about not failing. Their entire life is devoted to avoiding failure. Whatever it costs, whatever mental gymnastics are required, however strong the evidence to the contrary, men vehemently assert that they do not fail – in anything. They are great lovers, superlative wits, amazing drinkers, fantastic technicians, brilliant lateral thinkers, unbeatable sportsmen and undeniably clever at anything else that may be required of them. Therefore, they are indispensable to women, who have difficulties in all these fields.

To preserve this self-deception, men have to believe that there is more to them than there really is. Deep down they know they have not progressed mentally since the age of 15. All that has changed in adulthood is the type and extent of the mess and damage they leave behind them. They have abandoned their childhood toys for mobile phones, car stereo systems, the Internet, real guns, the Stock Market and women.

But, whatever men know deep down, they want women to believe that men are superior, so superior that they can laugh at the slogan that reads: 'Women like the simple things in life, like men.' It's a joke almost worthy of a man.

## FUNDAMENTAL DIFFERENCES

For decades, scientists, social reformers, and feminists have been arguing that men are pretty much the same as women. Men themselves, however, have tended to disagree, basing their opinion on the blindingly obvious (always their preferred method). The empirical observation of any adolescent boy in mirror sunglasses, groping his way along a nudist beach, is that men and women are manifestly not the same at all. And nor are their responses to one another.

We recommend that you tend towards this latter view. The retreat from hardcore 1970s feminism is in your favour: it is once more permissible to state openly, and in mixed company, that men and women are really quite different. However, your watchword in this argument should be moderation: gender stereotypes may be less extreme, subtler, and more diluted than in previous generations, but the sentiments expressed by this popular bumper sticker still prevail: 'Women who seek to be equal to men lack ambition.'

In other words, these days men can get away with less.

## Brawn

Men are built differently from women, which they are very happy to demonstrate at the drop of a hat, or any other item of clothing. They are also built differently from each other, though here it is usually a matter of quantity rather than quality.

There are several handy facts to keep at the ready as you go about your bluffing. (N.B. They are based on the average or mean, rather than the magnificent):

- Male babies are born bigger than female babies.

- Men are stronger than women. Nearly twice as much of their body is devoted to muscle tissue (average 57 lbs – about 26 kilos, compared with 33 lbs – 15 kilos).

- Men are 10% heavier and 7% taller than women.

- Men's main internal organs (heart, lungs, kidneys, waste-disposal units) are larger, and their bone structure is more massive.

- Men's brains are bigger, by about 5 oz (the weight of a generous apple), which is why they find using the whole brain at any one time more exhausting.

- Men can also run faster. They don't have airbags in the front seat.

There are physiological reasons for these differences. Men can run faster because their bodies contain a higher concentration of haemoglobin which carries oxygen in the blood, and the greater the concentration, the more quickly oxygen can be taken up in an active body. Men also run faster because they have a narrower pelvis, which means that when running they need to rotate it less fast than women in proportion to the distance covered. It also means that no man can walk like Marilyn Monroe.

We suggest, however, that you steer conversation away from the physical differences between men and women. They do not explain why men behave differently. The caveman analogy comes in handy at this point – and few men will take offence. Most will happily identify with cavemen, and rather wish they could be cavemen again, back in the days when things were much simpler.

In those days, b.c. (Before Contraception), women spent the greater part of their lives pregnant and child-rearing, and could not stray far from the cave. Men roamed around in packs, hunting wild animals for food and looking for trouble. They had to be physically tough to outwit their prey, and rivals who wanted access to their cave and their women. One should be careful not to make all this seem too idyllic.

Since early man bothered little with etiquette, it is likely that he feasted on mammoth rump steak, while early woman had to be content with chewing the hide. So man grew stronger, and woman grew weaker.

This basic modus vivendi took several million years to develop. You can point out that it hasn't evolved any further in the intervening aeons. In any case, modern culture still reinforces this attitude: men, rather than women, are the ones expected to fight wars, play rough sports and hit the burglar over the head with the poker.

There are plenty of vestiges of the caveman in modern man, and this is not just in his attitude to women. Men like to show off, beating their chests and hollering to demonstrate who dominates, and who has something to prove, before phoning their wife with what they hope will be a believable excuse for not coming home.

## Brain

Research into the brain reinforces the historical divergences between the sexes. These have been refined and honed over countless generations: those men not blessed with certain vital skills – or virtues – would not have lived long enough to reproduce and pass them on. It has been found that:

- men have greater spatial aptitudes: originally necessary for following bison over the grasslands, today evident in better map-reading skills and sense of orientation. In laboratory studies, men score over women in tests involving mazes and perspective – but then, so do rats.

- men have more precise target-directed motor skills, once vital for aiming javelins at mammoths from 100 paces, now displayed by a greater skill at reversing cars into small spaces, zapping warlords on play stations and throwing darts in the pub. Almost every game or sport played in the world today has been invented to emphasise male superiority, with the exception of synchronised swimming.

- in good light, men can pick out smaller objects in the distance, especially if they are moving – useful for bringing home the prime ingredients for hedgehog pie and avoiding police speedtraps.

- men can tolerate twice as much noise as women, and that is not just because they are making it.

It is generally, though grudgingly, agreed by men that women have the advantage with social skills and language. This is because of women's greater activity between the two hemispheres of the brain, and a larger concentration of cells in the region of the cortices associated with languages and listening.

If you wish to strike a contradictory note on this topic, offer the opinion that the lack of cross-currents between the hemispheres in men's brains may be to men's advantage. Poorer communication skills and a less developed sense of empathy help them to be more single-minded and more focused, and better suited to waging war and stripping lead off roofs, where being overly concerned about the consequences could be a distinct disadvantage.

## Blame testosterone

Virtually everyone – including men – agrees that men could behave better. Few, however, know the scientific basis for men's transgressions, so this is fertile ground for the bluffer. You can safely put your eggs in one basket: testosterone.

Testosterone is the male hormone produced by the testicles, and accounts for the development of the male sex organs in the womb and their subsequent development at puberty. The rest of the tale hangs from there, as it were.

Testosterone makes men masculine. It gives them:

- a deeper voice
- more body hair
- virility
- aggression
- that oddly gamey whiff to be savoured in any locker room – the one that is not related to sweaty trainers.

Testosterone helps to create the distinctively male brain. It affects the way the body reacts to stress and copes with adrenaline. Bristling with testosterone, men look for scary and exciting experiences, such as hurling themselves off heights on the end of elastic bands, kerb-crawling, and eating the hottest possible curry. Testosterone impels men to take risks. Men see this as a point in their favour since it makes them more predisposed than women to take up challenges, to clinch that billion-dollar deal, to reach the top of Mount Everest, to cross the Atlantic in a sieve, to make a pass at their best friend's wife. Unfortunately it also leads them into trouble. Men are more accident-prone than women; in fact, they are four times more likely to die in an accident.

Men's ability to judge distances when at the wheel, and to assess accurately the gaps between oncoming vehicles explains why men think they are better drivers than women. Paradoxically, because they think they are better drivers, and enjoy the testosterone-induced thrill of speed, they also drive faster. Insurance statistics show that 94% of serious accidents are caused by men.

Nowadays, testosterone is blamed for all manly misdeeds. Men are not entirely comfortable with this. It suggests they aren't responsible for their actions, which is how they prefer to view women – i.e., if anyone is hopelessly adrift in a sea of hormones, it is women, not men. Should you find yourself bluffing to such an intransigent male, silence him with the fact, incontrovertible even to men, that it is they who are responsible for the vast proportion of violent crime. When men are in their late teens and early twenties testosterone levels reach their peak, aggression comes to the fore and, for some, beating up rival football fans can be more thrilling than kicking the ball into a net.

Research among male football supporters shows that watching their team win can produce a 20% increase in testosterone levels, and that they will experience a testosterone surge merely by thinking about their team's forthcoming fixtures.

Both men and women possess varying amounts of testosterone and oestrogen. Medical tests carried out on violent women in U.S. jails show that they have higher than average levels of testosterone, another statistic to give the male hormone a bad name.

However, one advantage of testosterone, as any school teacher will tell you, is that it makes boys and men less susceptible to infestations of head lice.

## GROWING UP

Men don't grow up if they can possibly help it. The majority have to, however, and during this process suffer the following four stages:

### Boys will be boys

Boys become boys in the seventh week of pregnancy. At a critical moment, the vital 'Y' element of the male XY sex chromosome triggers a conversion process: the potentially female attributes of the foetus atrophy, the penis and the testes develop, and testosterone goes into full production.

If your taste is for high-risk bluffing, you may care to posit the argument that this detonation by the Y chromosome represents a positive act of divergence from the prototype; it suggests innate male dynamism, perhaps even superiority. But beware: you lay yourself open to the observation that it could also explain why there are more male transvestites than female – men have more female in them than women have male. We advise you to stick to research which indicates that boys show innately masculine behaviour when still in the womb. While female foetuses tend to move their lips, rehearsing their well-known talent for talk, unborn boys thrash their limbs about pretending to be astronauts in their own little private space capsule.

In the nursery and the playground, boys demonstrate early their propensity for noisy, rough-and- tumble, high-energy games. This is transmuted in later life to body-contact team sports. Boys pit themselves against each other with boxing, batting, and balls. They become expert at creating noise and making big expansive movements – imitating the sound of machine-gun fire as they fly hand-held plastic fighter planes around the garden in a dogfight with the cat.

Whereas girls will play quietly for hours with a toy put in front of them, boys will want to investigate everything in sight. But their innate inner drive dictates that they will soon be distracted and move on to something else. In later life this frequently takes a female form.

In one test arranged by sociologists, girls and boys were offered dolls to play with. The girls cuddled and talked to the dolls: the boys took their clothes off.

## Teenage man

All teenagers are misunderstood by adults, but male teenagers are misunderstood by female teenagers as well, and female teenagers are what matter to them most. The only time in his life that the male really tries to understand the female is when he is a teenager. After that, he will have had such a rough time being teased, taunted, unnerved and rejected, he may give up for ever. As far as men are concerned, teenage girls can be held totally responsible for men's eventual adult behaviour.

## Middle-age man

The seven-year itch, the eleven-year itch, and the mid-life crisis all occur between the mid-thirties and late forties. Thirty-nine is the worst age of all, when a man takes stock of what he has or has not achieved before being inevitably launched into the Over Forties. It is at about this time in his life that he gets bored with his job and worries that he is no longer attractive. ('I'm losing hair off my head', cries the anguished hero of *City Slickers*, 'and starting to get it in my ears and on my back. I'm starting to look like The Fly!') Middle-age man tries to reassure himself by flirting with secretaries and air stewardesses, is desperate if he fails and even more desperate if he succeeds because he is not at all ready to cope with the ensuing marital problems.

On the plus side, he is probably better off than ever, more self-assured, more confident, better at sex, and often, as a result, quite unbearable.

## Dirty old man

Though men have the advantage over women of being thought to get more attractive as they get older, old men become grumpy. This is apparently the effect of the gradual decrease in testosterone level, but it is also a by-product of the fact that all those urges and ambitions that once motivated them suddenly seem rather pointless.

Younger men are encouraged by the sight of old men marrying young women and siring children when well into their nineties: it gives them some hope of distant adventures. They are not aware of the effort this involves, nor the failure rate.

Men lose their fertility at a rate of about 12% per annum (cumulative, or index linked) from the age of 30. Testosterone diminishes with age, and with it goes not only their libido but also their sparkle. In the U.S., men anxious to avoid the embarrassment of impotence on a date have found it useful to stick a testosterone patch, similar to the smokers' nicotine patch, to remote parts of their anatomy. Neither party feels very flattered if this is

discovered.
# SEX

'A very marked difference between the sexes,' noted diarist Elizabeth Delafield in the 1930s, 'is the male tendency to procrastinate everything in the world except sitting down to a meal and going up to bed.' This is a chivalrous observation befitting its date. In reality, most men would unhesitatingly scrub round the meal if bed was in the offing.

Men are said to think of sex every six minutes – unless they are actually having sex, when to delay the final surge they think about real ale, the nine times table, or reinforced concrete construction.

After thinking about sex every six minutes for six days, men are beginning to need to do something about it. Any longer and they become like a bull elephant in musk – agitated, consumed by forces they only vaguely comprehend. They are often intensely grateful to women who take pity, and help them out. Few men can summon the objectivity of a committed misogynist, who complained of sex: 'the pleasure is momentary, the position ridiculous and the expense damnable.'

Men will do anything for sex, and will behave quite out of character to achieve it, such as spending several hours being romantic, and paying attention to what a woman says. A woman can probably persuade a man to undertake any favour against the promise of sex: put up a curtain rail, iron a shirt, ring the dentist...

Bluffing is often at its most effective when arguing against a received wisdom. If you know enough to achieve this, your audience will think you really must be in command of the subject. Accordingly, we counsel you to dismiss the 'men thinking with their testosterone is bad' thesis. Opine that men are simply the vehicles for the human urge to regenerate. Suggest that this is a bit of a burden, and given that sperm are produced from puberty onwards, something of a life sentence. Thus, since most men would happily cast their seed far and wide given half a chance, monogamy represents a serious sacrifice. It is said that in denying himself sex outside marriage, a man makes a biological sacrifice comparable to women having children.

Men are controlled and regulated by their sperm – masses of them clamouring to get out and reproduce at the earliest possible opportunity. Some 100 million are released on each ejaculation and only one is needed for successful fertilisation. Men never do things by halves.

## Selfish genes
Sperm are not overly fussy about how and when they get launched on their mission. Men can do the necessary in just about any circumstance you care to think of – except, perhaps, in front of a critical audience. However, the genes get a say in this.

Genes seem to have preferences – a phenomenon expressed as 'selfish'. Their agenda is to find the best partner with which to reproduce and ensure their survival. Men project the genes' preference, or the sexual urge, into women – metaphorically as well as literally. They have ways of verbalising the genes' preferences in such expressions as 'fwaw!', 'cor!', 'she's gorgeous'. This urge is sometimes called the 'genetic imperative'– a useful term to explain just about anything a man thinks or does.

It does not quite stop with sex. If it did, men would be concerned only with impregnating as many women as possible. What restrains them (most of them, anyhow) is the need to know that their offspring can be nurtured long enough to ensure a subsequent generation. Men may attempt to dress up their behaviour in any number of ways, but it always comes back to the genes. Never fear that your male bluffees will take offence at this analysis. Few, in fact, will object. It relieves them of responsibility.

They can look dispassionately upon the swelling evidence of their uncontrollable urges as an alien force, hold up their hands and declare with a shrug: 'Nothing to do with me.'

## Virginity

Peer group pressure makes virginity a burden and an embarrassment for men. For women there is at least some tradition of merit attached. The difficulty is finding someone with whom to dispose of it. It's a tough one. On the one hand, an adolescent male will do all he can to make out that he is an experienced lover, and the lie increases with age. On the other, he is certain that his first proper sexual encounter will be such a tidal wave of sensual experience that he is bound to make a complete hash of it. He knows the mechanics – he has studied this at length, and rehearsed it repeatedly. But the details remain obscure, and there is no way of predicting the input of the opposite party. It is liable to be a disaster.

This should not, of course, matter at all. But male pride comes into play here, of the obstinate and hard-boiled kind that is difficult to dislodge. Ideally the inexperienced male lover needs the reassurance of sympathy and patience, and preferably a sense of fun. Unfortunately, male talk and girls' teenage magazines suggest that no-one should be satisfied with anything less than sexual olympics and immediate multiple orgasms.

We cannot over-emphasise the need for tact when the conversation enters this territory. The odds are that at least one of the men you're addressing will have insecurities about his early sex life. Exacerbate these and you will antagonise him; an inconsiderate bluffer is a self-defeating bluffer. Gently throw in a mention of surveys which suggest that no less than 25%, if not 40% (truth is a victim here), of men entering university are virgins. And that roughly the same number are virgins when they leave.

It is easy enough to spot a virgin. Most men will talk frankly and honestly (male-speak for boasting) to other men about their sexual encounters. The virgin will remain quiet. Instruction isn't practice, and he just cannot confidently imagine what it is really like. His mind reels at the very idea, and he is not sure he has the vocabulary.

Young men dream of being shown the way to pleasure and bliss by an experienced older woman – just like The Graduate. As Mae West put it: 'Men like women with a past because they hope history will repeat itself.'

## Equipment

From infancy, boys learn that their penis has a life of its own – activity associated with mysterious and pleasurable feelings. Dangling so prominently, it has a permanent presence, is readily to hand, and seldom out of mind.

The penis is the male organ par excellence. Men are so obsessed by this possession that they regard it as a pet and converse with it. This no doubt explains why it has so many pet names (see Glossary).

When aroused, it is operated entirely by hydraulics, the effect of blood being pumped into it. With nerve endings concentrated near the tip, it is a strange combination of rubbery inertness and sensitivity.

Worshipped by Hindus as a 'lingam', or symbol of Shiva, and by the Romans who made a fertility symbol out of the enormously well-endowed god Priapus, it is disconcerting for men to discover that modern women are not so impressed by their pride and joy. Indeed, many of them find the penis absurd, hilarious, downright ugly, and certainly over-ambitious. Ridicule is one way to ensure that it fails to rise to its proper function.

As for the accompanying accoutrements, the testicles,

by contrast, are as fragile as eggshells. A sharp knock or tap can induce excruciating pain, even retching, to a degree no woman can fully appreciate. Not for nothing have these been singled out as the male weak spot, conveniently located for kicking or kneeing. They represent a major design fault, or evidence that God is a woman.

## Size

Most men are secretly concerned about the size of their appendage, especially in the years before it has been put to the test. They are constantly told that size does not matter – 'It's not how big it is, it's what you do with it' – but it still bothers them. They hear worrying stories of some women who cannot be satisfied with anything less than Michelangelo's David, full scale. On the other hand, those who conclude by furtive glances in communal showers that theirs is above average, can harbour fears that their car may be too big for the garage.

The relaxed penis can be any size, depending on the ambient temperature. Cold induces unflattering shrivelling: this is why, at nudist beaches, men walk quickly towards their towels after swimming.

In erect form, size averages out. By producing statistics here, you can significantly boost your image as an 'expert' on men. The figures are guaranteed to provoke lively (and in all probability ribald) discussion, and people tend to perceive a correlation (correctly or otherwise) between how much a teacher has entertained them and how much he or she knows. The average size of an erect penis in Europe, you can mention nonchalantly, is 6 inches; in Asia 5; and in Africa 7. Before anyone produces a ruler, you can remind your audience that the average duration of intercourse for an orang-utan is 15 minutes, with a penis of just 1½ inches*.

* In metric: 152 mm, 127 mm, 178 mm, 38 mm, respectively.

## Masturbation

Just about every man masturbates, from about the age of 12 onwards. It is through 'playing with himself' that a boy will first discover erections and, by persistent stroking, one day or night the world will suddenly turn inside out, as an extraordinary, dynamic sensation fills his entire body and produces a mysterious dollop of goo. Nothing quite prepares a male for this moment, and he will probably remember the time and place of it for the rest of his life.

Boys and men will go on practising for the real thing throughout adolescence and into adulthood. There is a physical need to discharge a build-up of sperm, which if not resolved will express itself as an involuntary 'wet dream' during sleep.

Masturbation is often accompanied by a slight sense of guilt, as is any solitary indulgence. But no-one really believes it is a sin any more, makes you blind or that it can put spots on your upper arms. 'Don't knock it,' said Woody Allen in *Annie Hall*, 'it's sex with someone you love.'

## Performance

Premature ejaculation is the great male fear. The trouble is that coming too soon is a fact of life. It is not sperms' duty to hang about, and they require a fair amount of training to induce them to delay. Surveys have revealed that 75% of men ejaculate within two minutes of penetration. Some even jump the starting gun.

As with virginity, you must take great care not to alienate insecure males among your listeners. We suggest that you take the pressure off them (as it were) by referring to the conflicting sexual demands placed on them by their partner. Women, and in particular young women, demand foreplay to stimulate arousal as they seek to find the best route to pleasure. But all the time foreplay is going on, the sperm are massing on the starting line. This mismatch requires negotiation, time and perseverance to resolve – not qualities readily associated with the quenching of mutual lust. Condoms are the silver lining to the dual clouds of infection and conception: they desensitise men, so women have a better prospect of increased duration.

There is only one thing more worrying for men than coming too soon: total mechanical failure. This may be brought on by an attack of anxiety, fear of failure, an excess of Dutch courage, or the natural built-in obsolescence of age. The high statistical occurrence of 'erectile dysfunction' which is said to affect one in every two men aged 40–70, has been outed by the worldwide success of the stiffening drug Viagra, boosted by the advertisements of Brazilian football star Pele (born 1940) along with puns from the press about balls, and rising to the task of conquering the taboo.

For men, orgasm is the raison-d'être of sex. They assume therefore that this is also the case for women, and cannot quite believe that women can be satisfied with less. Mutual orgasm represents the zenith of male sexual ambition – not a bad goal to aim at, but in reality, a difficult one to score. As a butler prone to keyholes once put it, 'Gentlemen often have more enthusiasm than skill.'

## Libido

All men are chancers: the male sexual drive is strong enough to lead even TV evangelists astray. Some 25% of married men have had at least one extramarital affair – and this figure is based on those who admit to it. There are also plenty who prefer to believe that sex without penetration does not count.

Women tend to leave their husbands for someone else because they have reached the end of their tether; marital love has keeled over and seems impervious to revival. Men, on the other hand, often see an affair as a bit of an adventure to spice up their lives, to shore up their flagging egos. It does not mean that their love for their wife has evaporated, just that it is not all-consuming. There is some spare capacity (all those sperms swarming for migration), and someone has come into their lives who can give them a home. They will often be happy to motor along like this until one or other woman decides she no longer wants a part-timer.

Until viruses received wide publicity, it was generally considered acceptable for men to sleep around, especially in their youth. But there was a downside to this licence to bonk. It meant that even very young men could never admit that they hadn't had experience of sex. And this has led to the curse of the Burden of Sexual Experience. All men have to pretend they are sexual rogues, and not just to each other.

Women are party to this dreadful deceit. A husband who is seen as reliably faithful may be seen as a little dull – possibly even unattractive. It used to be the case among the French bourgeoisie that a husband who did not have a mistress was something of a social embarrassment. However, rogue males do not want to be confronted by rogue females because:

- they are demoralized by women who are more sexually experienced than they are. It can lead to comparisons, and all comparisons are odious.
- they want to control a woman's sexuality to avoid any suspicion that they may be raising someone else's progeny.
- they take a dim view of women who behave as badly as

they do.
## Pornography

Many women find pornography baffling. Men don't. For bluffers trying to account for this conundrum, there is an agreeably neat explanation: women are turned on by what is done to them, men are turned on by what they see. Almost all men enjoy eroticism, and always have. They fantasise about sex all the time, so it is not difficult to market fantasy to them.

They profess to find sex videos and magazines inspiring, exciting and a little daring – it's rather like the first time they use a grown-up swear word: they are aware that this is something powerful, but don't really understand what it means.

When pressed about their attitude to pornography, men wilt. They surrender the first untenable position (that pornography is art), and take up a second indefensible position (that pornography is just a bit of fun). From this point it's not long before they retreat to a third position (that it doesn't do any harm), and a fourth (well, yes, all right then, it's demeaning), and a fifth (look, can't we talk about something else?). It is not an heroic defence, and it's a tragic certainty that, with the publication of the next day's pin-up, the same men will repeat the whole process.

However, the publishers of images of women with ginormous breasts are peddling an ancient myth that men necessarily like that kind of thing. Women who are less well endowed can sleep easier on this one – and probably do.

## Prostitution

Men are perfectly capable of regarding sex in a totally impersonal way, and keeping it in a different compartment from notions such as love, family, or fishing. It is this disposition that leads men to seek gratification from prostitutes. Some men will argue that prostitution serves a valid function. It is a therapy; it services a male need by means of a neutral commercial transaction, which would probably otherwise have to be satisfied by less willing partners elsewhere; and like so many illicit things, it is also fun.

For balanced bluffing, however, it's advisable that you mention some of the counter-arguments, such as health and safety, and terms of contract. But never redundancy payments.

## FEELINGS

It is, of course, a cheap joke to suggest that the very idea of men's feelings is a contradiction in terms. Men do have feelings, and they are not just all over their body.

The trouble is they are brought up to deny feelings, to bury them, in non-Latin countries anyway. Parents and peers train them not to show emotion, so that when deeply moved, they will turn to something intensely distracting – like ping-pong, horseplay, or pot-holes. When the Japanese head of a collapsed business or the Australian Prime Minister breaks rank and bursts into tears, it becomes headline news. The upshot of such sublimation is that men are more likely than women to suffer depression and have a 400% higher suicide rate.

### Approval

Men are suckers for approval. A nod and a smile go a long way to winning the male heart. They want to feel that women have noticed them and that women need them.

Best of all would be if women admired them. They would also like to feel that women trusted them, but that's probably hoping for too much.

Men would be putty in women's hands if they were given the eye-sparkling, adoring look of Ingrid Bergman in *Casablanca*, or the eye-smouldering one of Lauren Bacall in *To Have and Have Not* just before she says 'If you want anything, just whistle...' It is when they yearn for this approval that men are at their most dog-like and appealing.

It has been a source of much anguish to men that women have discovered how much men long to be admired. Traditionally it was all the other way round – women pined for men's attention, affection, adoration. Men galloped by, scarcely noticing them, unless they needed rescuing. Today, women seldom need rescuing and men have traded in their steeds. This is complete gender reversal. Jane Austen has been swapped for Jackie Collins, and men are left to create new roles for themselves. Men now have to work far harder to earn that treasured approval, making the best job of it they can, with inadequate props.

## Independence

Men are admired if they are independent, competent, self-sufficient, and if they do not match up to this they feel something of a failure. Their sense of independence is an important factor in their relationships. Women are likely to define themselves in terms of their chosen loved one; men are apt to see their loved one as a partner who might be cherished, but who does not redefine them.

An interesting by-product of this is that men prefer to feel that they are paying their way in a relationship. This fact is of particular value to the bluffer as it is very simple to work into conversation in a restaurant or bar. Men have to feel competent, they have to be the provider. This is the hunter instinct, an old habit that is taking a long time to die. Funnily enough, women do not seem to mind this.

By contrast, house-husbands who stay at home while their wives go out to work are still very much in the minority. They are readily identifiable because they see themselves as unusual, look faintly bruised and typically make elaborate justifications – usually 'economic circumstances' – as to why they are not pursuing a more conventional career.

At all times men like keeping their options open. It is all part of their urgent need for independence and to be seen to be independent, even if it makes them seem obstinate and foolish. Press them too hard and they will feel their options closing down. It is a fatal error to box a man into a corner. But give him the opportunity to say no, and he is more likely to say yes.

## Pride

Men like to be right. In general, if they say they admire a woman with ideas, they mean a woman who shares their ideas. Women find it is often best to tell men that they are right even if, patently, they are not: there is little value in arguing. (Overheard from a man, expressed with the greatest conviction: 'I know I'm right – and if I'm not, it's a mistake.')

By the same token, men do not like to be contradicted: it is an assault on their fragile integrity. They cannot bear to be thought ineffectual or inadequate, and will avoid any situation which insinuates that they need help. You can advance this theory by using an example that everyone will recognise: men hate having to ask for directions from strangers. They would rather drive around a city with a car full of scratchy children for hours, getting ever later for lunch, than wind down the window and ask the way. It looks too much as if they don't know.

All men realise that this instinct is absurd, but male pride is stronger than reason.

## Stubbornness

Bluffers are under some obligation to point out that it is quite wrong to think of men as stubborn. They are not stubborn, and there is absolutely no point in suggesting that they are.

Men pride themselves on being tolerant, flexible, accommodating and forgiving, especially towards women. Saying that they are stubborn, intransigent, obstinate, or downright impossible, is evidence of a clear and simple failure to appreciate the masculine virtues of self-assurance, confidence, decisiveness, persistence and dogged determination.

The argument is cut and dried; the case is closed. Men are not stubborn, and there is no way anyone is going to shift them from that point of view.

## Socialising skills

You may, on the other hand, concede that men are less socially adept than women. Evidence comes not just from casual observation, but also from brain scans and genetic research.

It has been discovered that only females are born with a 'switched on' socialising gene. It seems that males are not born with any genetically inherited socialising skills at all; they have to learn them.

This means that men are less aware of other people's feelings, oblivious to the effects of their behaviour, and difficult to reason with when upset; less pleasant altogether than women, poor things. Nor are they intuitive. Men don't even have enough intuition to realise how much intuition women have.

Men believe that when women complain, or talk about a problem, they are demanding that men do something about it. Women don't always want something done. Often they want sympathy and comfort. But men would need intuition to know that.

Before incorporating this topic into your bluffing, you must be warned that when confronted with these biological facts, men exhibit one of two responses:

1  Arrogance, since it gives them a cast-iron excuse for behaving as they do.

2  Pique, because it puts them on the defensive, and men do not like to be seen at a disadvantage, or lacking in anything, in any field, ever.

If you get the first response, sit back and laugh with the rest of the group. If you get the second, have a crumb of comfort ready to offer to the disconcerted man. Assure him that it is not the mother who passes on the socialising genes to her daughter, but the father.

## Conversation

The average woman uses 10,000 words a day in speech; the average man finds 4,000 perfectly adequate. Around the house, men's conversation is especially economical, often reduced to grunts and utterances of one syllable. For them, telephone calls are for the transmission of information, not for gossiping or the exchange of confidences.

Men have one fear greater than being proved wrong: being thought weak. In conversation with women, they generally tell their listeners what they think they want to hear. Their conversational strategy is devised to disguise their vulnerability. This has an intimidating effect on them as well. Men with low self-esteem worry about why the world isn't revolving around them. Confident men cannot help thinking that it does.

The confident man can dominate the conversation at a dinner party, brag about his achievements, attempt to cap the last story, and steer the discussion. If he is in an ebullient mood, he expects everyone to follow suit. As a result there is a fair chance that the atmosphere will be combative, stimulating, enlightening and amusing.

It could also be a crashing bore. But men have the antidote to this. They don't listen. They are too busy thinking what they are going to say next. It can come as a complete surprise to them to find someone with something sufficiently interesting to say to interrupt their thought processes.

The corollary of this, which is that women are attracted to men who are good at listening, can be a very handy tool as you conduct your bluffing. If one of your male listeners is talking too much, slip into the conversation the fact that accomplished seducers cultivate the virtue of listening well. You will find that he pipes down after that.

## Opinions

Men feel obliged to have an opinion about everything. Being asked for their opinion is the one thing they are guaranteed to hear.

Even if they don't have much of one, they will want to express it. In many, as soon as a thought pattern flows through their brain it will start heading for the mouth, and will pour forth without hindrance, and regardless of whether others are talking at the time. (Men are great interrupters – though they have cunningly created the

25

belief that interrupting is a female trait.) Many have learnt to withstand this impulse, but any delay tends to result in an even weightier pronouncement when it is released.

Men's pride does not allow them to be less knowledgeable than women. They therefore go to great lengths to make sure that they are well versed in any subject which might come up during a party, conference, car journey, flight, picnic. They are incurable purchasers of reference books, dictionaries and encyclopædias. The Bluffer's Guides were invented by a man.

## Buddies

Male friendships are centred round activities. Not for them cosy, supportive gossiping simply because 'it's good to talk'. When buddies meet, even after an absence of ten years, they are more likely to discuss last night's television than the failed marriages, horrendous surgery, bankruptcies or other tragedies that have struck them since they were last together.

So their buddies are people with like-minded interests – sailing, golfing, gardening, drinking, bird-watching – people with whom they do things, rather than talk about them. They muddle along with these chums comfortably when their pursuits coincide. They may even end up with a deep bond but, on the whole, friendship is not a question of baring their souls.

Most men tend not to develop close friends after the formative years of their lives – notably university. They are just too busy, too active, too mobile, too tied up with their work to make the effort. Their social lives increasingly revolve around their wives' friends, and the husbands of their wives' friends. The result is that the majority tend to end up with the diminishing number of buddies they started with, and many end up with few to speak of. Or to.

## Chauvinism

Male Chauvinists like being called Male Chauvinists. They take it as a compliment, not an insult.

They may be an outrageous and unacceptable figure in the modern age, but they cannot be written off completely. To every male trying to soothe the screaming baby with a bottle of expressed milk comes that momentary flash of envy and doubt when he thinks that perhaps the Chauvinist has got things just about right: no principles, no conscience, no housework, no danger of disappointed expectations – and, believe it or not, no shortage of female admirers.

## Commitment

Men find it hard to commit themselves to a relationship. Getting them to do so is like getting hold of the soap in the bath.

A sense of commitment to a partnership – or rather the lack thereof – is one factor you can safely cite as the key difference between men and women. For men the very idea of commitment is uncomfortable: 'to commit' after all is the same verb used of suicide, or being sent to an asylum. Marriage also goes by the unnerving term 'wedlock'.

'A man is incomplete until he has married. Then he is finished,' said Zsa-Zsa Gabor, after considerable research. Men harbour the distinct fear that marriage will change them. Women simply hope it will.

A key factor in persuading people of your expertise is how much highly-charged debate you can engender. And few debates have a higher charge than those you will engender by stating that, like other primates, men are not essentially monogamous, and the chances are that they will not be able to satisfy their sexual drives in one relationship. Current divorce rates of one in three in the U.K. and one in two in the U.S. would seem to be evidence of this.

Monogamy presents men with a real problem. They believe there is something unnatural about it. Although it is practised by 90% of bird species, only 3% of mammals are monogamous – and men see themselves more as gorillas than mistle thrushes.

Since men like to keep their options open, they like to think that there are ways to preserve their independence, even in the heart of a happy marriage. 'The sea is like a wife,' runs an old northern Spanish saying, 'she entices you, draws you in, then kills you' – a little strong, but the Spanish love anything that promises death. Men do see marriage as an end as much as a beginning. They try to guard against this by secretly holding on to far more of their former single way of life than women do.

On the other hand, men also accept marriage as a sensible compromise with joys of its own. There are a number of pay-offs to long-term commitment, such as:

– domestic comfort
– a captive audience
– increased tax allowance
– better catering arrangements.

A married man envies the single man on Saturday nights, but not on Sunday morning.

# ATTITUDES TO ...

## Women

Secretly, men think women are cleverer than they are, but convention does not allow them to admit it. In fact, men and women share the same average IQ. When this was revealed to the world in 1912, the male world was publicly shocked, but privately greatly relieved – they had no idea they were that smart.

Surveys, always trusty and hard-working pixies for any bluffer, can be especially useful here. Tell your listeners that in surveys, men consistently overestimate their IQs (knowing that they are doing so), while women underestimate theirs (not knowing that they are doing so). Among couples, despite huge evidence to the contrary, the majority of women will state that their partner is the more intelligent of the two, and children of either sex will tend to say their father is more intelligent than their mother.

One of the smarter members of your audience may suggest that one interpretation of this is that more intelligent women do not have husbands, or partners or children. You must be prepared for this. Answer that the statistics do not support that reckoning – even though, you can add with a professorial air, there are 105 women to every 100 men in the Western world. The clue to the riddle, you can reveal, lies in the word 'intelligent': women are happy to settle for being considered equally capable. They know that most men are daunted by intelligent women, and to accommodate this, deliberately 'dumb themselves down'.

Men may say that they like independent women with ambition, who are self-confident, going places, but in practice they prefer women who do not challenge their 'top dog' status in the household, or in an area of expertise they consider their own.

A man dominated by his wife is considered weak – by

women too. Both sexes tend to think that a household where the 'woman wears the trousers' is some kind of aberration, inviting pity for the poor hen-pecked male, and a fair amount of jocularity. This concept is very rarely heard in the reverse; no surprise or ridicule is expressed when a wife is dominated by her husband. This is as it should be, of course.

Men might try to shift the blame for any unacceptably prejudiced views about women on to historical precedents. It was Aristotle who said: 'Man is by nature superior, and the female inferior: the one rules and the other is ruled.' And St Paul, no less, wrote in his Epistles to Timothy: 'Women are seen as unsuitable to teach or to have authority over men on the grounds that it was a woman, Eve, who introduced sin into the world.' Sadly, Timothy never wrote back to point out that 'it taketh two to tango'.

## Beauty

Men are genetically programmed to be attracted to beautiful women. They cannot resist. A male praying mantis is attracted to the most alluring female praying mantis – even though she is going to devour him alive while mating.

Beauty is a devastating force, so devastating that it is quite capable of reducing men to gibbering, stumbling, compliant wrecks. Despite all their fantasising, they are actually intimidated by great beauty, and often do not know how to behave when confronted by it. They are more at ease ogling at it on Page 3, or from the safe distance of a cinema seat.

There is a tradition among East Anglian chicken catchers (men who catch chickens for slaughter) that the attractiveness of a woman can be assessed in terms of pints of beer. The system is simple: the more attractive the woman, the fewer pints will be needed to summon up the necessary enthusiasm to commit carnal bliss with her. Some women might be flattered to know that they have been rated 'five-pinters' or even 'four-pinters'. However, after five pints of East Anglian ale most men are incapable of the carnal act anyway.

Real, live, accessible, very beautiful women are in any case rare. Men generally have to settle for something less – though it is probably not half as great a compromise as his opposite number may be making.

## Love

A man experiences love like any other creature: that is, the quickening of the heartbeat, the fresh sense of élan and renewal, the pleasure of intimacy and spontaneous understanding, the inspiration that drives him to put on a clean pair of socks.

He knows he is in love when he finds himself thinking not just about sex every six minutes, but about sex every six minutes with the same woman.

The difference is that men seem to need to be in love rather less than women do before committing themselves to sex. Women would be wise to take any man's profession of love with a pinch of salt. He is likely to be confusing love with lust. If he says 'I love you,' he probably means 'I want sex with you at the earliest possible opportunity.' It's the testosterone again, which may in fact be causing him to make a genuine error, rather than commit to an act of dishonesty. 'But yesterday you swore you'd love me for ever,' complains the jilted girl to her two-timing Lothario. 'I meant it at the time,' he replies.

There are plenty of advertisements for fragrances featuring a beautiful young woman and an (allegedly) stunning young man, both in a state of ecstasy supposedly brought on by the fragrance in question. Men look at the picture of the woman and think, 'She imagines it's for ever.' Then they look at the man and think, 'Rat'.

## Fatherhood

Men have got quite good at fatherhood. Even before their role kicks in, they will attend maternity classes, change the cassette tapes during the birth to provide some suitable background music, and offer encouragement at the head end if they can prevent themselves from passing out. You might like to refer to the survey in which 59% of new mothers declared that their husbands had been supportive. And then move quickly on before anyone can speculate about the remaining 41%.

These days men also do a great deal on the domestic front to help rear the children – like putting an announcement of the birth in one of the national newspapers. Men love children, but few share many women's delight at every primitive offering from the mewling, puking babe. Not until the child is capable of losing to them at football are men really interested in their offspring.

## Feminism

For a while, men faced an even more disturbing threat than the man-eating female: the man-hating female. It was a fairly terrifying experience, a bit like wrestling with an electric fence. There was no place a decent man could put himself without being labelled a 'typical male', the most hurtful of insults.

Fortunately, the spectre of radical feminism has withdrawn from the mainstream. At least men can now join a dinner party without fearing that they might be sitting down with the enemy.

We hesitate to offer an absolute guarantee on this, but it is fairly safe to assume for the purposes of your bluffing that extreme feminism is now regarded as 'old-fashioned'. Even feminist icons such as Professor Camille Paglia have been known to say that men are partly responsible for the civilisation that has given freedom to women – a heresy in previous eras.

Radical feminism contained rather too many home truths for comfort. Men are well aware of their shortcomings, and it bemuses them that women generally are so tolerant of them. By the law of opposites, this tolerance can excite male resentment, and is said to be a cause of misogyny.

Some men believe that feminism heralds the end of civilisation as we know it. They blame it for the collapse of family values, the increase in single-parent families, divorce, dysfunctional youth, violent crime and pot noodles. Professor Francis Fukuyama (a name to be handled with care) shows how many of society's ills have grown in parallel to the rise of feminism since the 1960s. He calls this effect 'The Great Disruption'. Societies which have maintained traditional male-female roles, like Japan, have not been visited by such moral decline, mainly because a woman dependent on her husband's income is likely to have the stability of the family at heart. Japanese women are not yet in a position to argue.

However, most men's attitudes to feminism remain ambivalent. They can be summed up by the equivocal statement: 'All women become like their mothers. That's their tragedy. No man does. That's his.'

# FOIBLES

## Wolf-whistling

The male habit of wolf-whistling is based on the tragic
misconception that women enjoy such signs of appreciation from strangers, and might even be attracted to the
wolf.

A feature of wolf-whistling which is little-noticed (and
therefore will do wonders for your image as an authority)
is that it is a group activity. A lone male never wolf-whis-
tles. He is usually one of a pack of three or more, often at
the safe distance of high-rise scaffolding or moving traffic.
The wolf-whistler is, in fact, not so much trying to attract
the female, as trying to impress his mates.

## Spitting

Football players do it, runners do it, even tennis players do
it on the green swards of Wimbledon. Men seem to believe
that spit cannot be swallowed. The challenge of hitting an
echoing spittoon in Westerns is probably more at fault
than anything. But it may be that, like all male animals
marking their patch, it is an ancient territorial instinct.

## Flies

It is a perpetual concern to men that their flies might be
open. They cannot bear the thought of the humiliation if
their underpants or, heaven forbid, the family crown
jewels were exposed to view. Better the earth should open
up and swallow them than that they should leave themselves open to the charge of 'being in a state of undress',
'flying low', or 'not pulling the curtains'.

Italian men surreptitiously touch their balls when they

pass a nun in the street, a superstition designed to ward off any threat to their fertility. Most men touch their flies surreptitiously when leaving the loo, to make sure all is safely battened down. Only macho man likes to leave the loo first, and then tug at his zip as though practising for the Olympic Weight Lifting Championships.

## Leaving the seat up

Life for a man would be a lesser experience if he was not able to unzip his trousers at the edge of the road and pee with glorious abandon into the open countryside. Men were born to urinate standing up, and stand-up urinals best serve this purpose. Sit-down W.C.s are poorly designed for a man, who cannot but help causing some collateral dispersal at this kind of height. It is a mistake to carpet a lavatory.

It is for this reason that a gentleman will always lift the seat. The fact that he is incapable of remembering to put it down again is a permanent irritation to women. 'The seat's up. Dad's home.'

Being able to pee standing up (whether from the stirrups or over the side of a yacht) is the one thing women envy about men. Men tend to keep quiet about their conduit's one imperfection. No matter how much it is shaken, there is always one last drop left in the pipeline.

## Sulking

Since men don't, won't or can't talk about emotional matters, they rarely solve an issue by discussing it. Instead they will go into a sulk, cradling their hurt feelings like a small furry animal. They will lapse into a moody silence, broken only by the occasional grunt, or rustle of newspaper. This bad mood may last for days, or even years.

Your male bluffees will be grateful when you point out that they're not to be blamed for sulking. (Your female ones won't, but at least you can rely on them not sulking about it.) Men's heroes and role models have eschewed talking and plumped for direct action. When did anyone ever see John Wayne counselling the Apache, Bruce Willis adopting a therapeutic attitude to Mafia hoods, or Sean Connery conducting a consciousness-raising session with SMERSH?

And men should be given credit for the magnanimous way in which they emerge from their sulk – head hanging, still muttering, ready to forgive their female partner the minute she admits it was all her fault. (Men are at their best when graciously pardoning and forgiving.)

There are two ways to deal with sulking men:

- ignore them and wait; or

- attempt to go into a parallel sulk to show them what it's like to live with.

Psychotherapists, you can mention in a casual way, say the first option is the wisest. Then moving from 'casual' to 'world-weary', you can add that they are probably hoping to gain two clients instead of one.

## Jokes

Men are better than women at storing the fund of jokes which is in perpetual motion round pubs and parties. It's a good way of ensuring that most precious of social rewards: approval. They are perhaps less inclined to admit that there is one more relevant reason, that men need jokes as reserve stock for conversation when sport fails.

## Hobbies

Men are super-active or think they should be. Every moment of the day must be put to good use, so hobbies were invented to occupy their minds during the long periods when they have absolutely nothing to do.

Hobbies annex most of men's spare time and cover a multitude of amazing displacement activities, from building cathedrals out of matchsticks to collecting beermats, old typewriters, hip-flasks, used flashbulbs, calculators which have given up the ghost, and pieces of string too short to use. Pointing this out is an example of that most welcome of creatures, the self-fulfilling bluff. At least one male in your audience will hear the word 'hobby' and automatically launch into an exhaustive account of his own. As detail upon detail tumbles from his tedious lips, everyone else will look upon you with respect that increases by the second.

## Sheds

Terminology is always helpful in creating the illusion that you know what you're talking about. Lightly toss in the phrase 'garden shed syndrome', following it up with the explanation that it's what psychologists call a man's innate need to establish his private territory.

Men adore their sheds. Here they can potter around in their old clothes, among tobacco tins filled with miscellaneous screws, and boxes of brackets and bits of twine, humming tunelessly to themselves, breathing in the homely smell of creosote and old flower pots, and perhaps snoozing in a battered old armchair. It is a haven, a comfort zone of their very own.

Their wives should not be jealous – many people pay good money for this kind of therapy.

## Tinkering with cars

Men have to have their toys: laptops, gliders, power drills, power boats, fishing rods, indoor putting kit, trouser press. The most ubiquitous of these is, of course, the car. Women have cars too, but they don't spend their leisure hours tinkering with them – rubbing them sensually with soft cloths, mending them, or stripping them and filling the garage with oily parts.

At the onset of their mid-life crisis, along with the desire to recapture their lost youth, comes a yearning for the sexy, sleek, high-performance car of their dreams – the menoporsche. But men are touchy about glib references to phallic symbols (even if the car is bright red and called a Probe). They do not see cars as 'penis substitutes' for two reasons:

1   Few men can afford a Lexus or a Ferrari.

2   There is no substitute for a penis.

# PRACTICALITIES

## Men at work

Men are apt to define themselves by their work – a rather tragic state of affairs given the extraordinary amount of dull labour that is required to keep the world turning. When a man talks to another man, he is dying to know first and foremost what the other one does, so that he can place him. Otherwise he is at a bit of a loss.

But you must remember, as you engage a man in conversation, that it is simply not allowed to ask him directly, 'what do you do ?' Certainly men themselves never operate like this. Instead, they tease the information from each other by talking about everything else – golf, cars, football, insurance – constantly looking for clues. When they have discovered the other one's profession, they can relax; then go through the conversation all over again and actually listen to what is being said.

At work, men have to treat other men carefully. They have to establish an understanding that suggests 'I'm not a threat to you, so let's work together and get the job done'. Otherwise there is hostility, and the next thing is they are outside with their antlers locked.

Men's obsession with work means that they are particularly prone to crisis on being made redundant: it is not just their job that has gone, but their vision of themselves as individuals.

In these days of sexual equality in the workplace it is dangerous to suggest that men are better than women in any particular field – although quite permissible to trumpet the reverse. It doesn't really matter, however, as men are powerful self-deceivers and great believers in what other men say. So, even though all men may know they are inferior to women, as long as other men say they are superior, that will be enough to restore their self-confidence.

Another area in which men appear to have the edge, and both male and female employers seem to agree, is risk-taking. Women bosses, for instance, often prefer male assistants because they will make decisions off their own bat and take the initiative to get things done. Risk of disapproval is involved. Successful risk-taking often makes the difference in advancing a business. Of course, there is also a downside: catastrophe.

Sadly, for most men work usually takes precedence over the family. Even if it's not in their original game plan, it just seems to happen, sidling up to them and then hijacking them. They pretend to be happy to leave the home early and return late, but this is just another example of men's amazing ability to deceive themselves. They may creep into a pub and assert to their mates that they'd rather be sharing a pint than reading bedtime stories to their children, but only a mate on a similar self-deceiving binge would believe them. If you're confident that your discussion is in a phase light-hearted enough to cope with this, you can mention the tragic truth that many men often only start to see their children on access weekends after the divorce.

## Domesticity

It is hard for a man to substitute a woman for the domestic virtues of bachelor life, the manly pleasures of:

- leaving the bed unmade
- belching ad lib
- using every pot in the kitchen.

Your bluffees may scoff when you assert that men are no less capable of looking after the home than women. But that scoff is an investment well worth your making. Let their derision abate, and point them to the evidence. It is widely accepted, for instance, that landlords prefer to have single men as tenants, because they keep the place looking reasonably tidy, even a little unoccupied. Also, single men often resent sharing a house with single women, who leave their undies soaking in the washbasin, use more loo paper, and treat the house as a changing-room. Your words will have all the more effect for having proved such an unlikely proposition. This is the bluffing equivalent of walking on water, and will establish you as an expert no-one dares challenge

You must also, however, have comments ready to keep

the women you're addressing on board. Surveys, for instance, have shown that, in couples where both partners are working, women still do six hours more housework per week. This may mean that only six hours of housework are being done in all. Such statistics reflect traditional divisions of labour by gender. But they may also relate to the fact that domestic chores tend to be done by the person with the greater sensitivity to dirty loos, grimy baths, sticky lino and overflowing laundry-baskets – and this is usually a woman. Men have the advantage of being thick-skinned; they approach the state of the house rather like the Three Wise Monkeys – see no evil, feel no evil, smell no evil.

Any woman prepared to see just how filthy a man would allow his home to be before he did anything about it, would have to wait a long time. Quentin Crisp once remarked that the nice thing about doing no housework is that after three years there doesn't seem to be any observable increase in the dust. This was one of the rare occasions when he spoke for almost all men.

But men have an increasingly uneasy attitude to housework. They don't mind leaving it undone, but they feel decidedly guilty if their female partner does it all. New Man likes to do his share. This usually means 'helping with' the washing up, the hoovering, and taking the smaller rubbish bin to the bigger one outside. The unspoken message is clear. It's still all the duty of the woman, but the male lends an occasional hand.

## Working with women

Men are coming to terms with having women as colleagues at work and even accepting them as seniors.

This does not come easily. Men are used to ruling the roost in the workplace: they have been doing so for thousands of years. It accounts for many of the traditional male attitudes which irk their female associates, principally:

- allowing the sight of a short skirt to affect their decisions;
- leaving all the lights blazing;
- expecting their own views to hold sway.

Men realise that there are many aspects of business which women do better than them. But they make these concessions from a position of strength. Statistics show that 89% of managers are men, so women have still not broken through the 'glass ceiling' sufficiently to challenge men at the top. But then men do not incubate human beings nor, for the most part, run homes or rear families. A suitably cynical note to strike here is that this arrangement is a great relief: otherwise what chance would they have?

It is said that men are better suited to the cut and thrust of the workplace. Apart from having more muscle, they have been trained on the school sports field to be team players, and to look up to the captain.

Because the area in the brain which produces sympathy is less active in men, they are better able to cope with confrontation, to hire and fire. But though this gave them a head start, the working world has changed to one in which traditional female virtues of communication and mutually beneficial compromise are increasingly valued. Men are having to adapt. (This does not mean they are willing to learn how to put new paper in the photocopier. Such roles are assigned to women – along with collecting their dry cleaning, selecting birthday cards for their wives, and ignoring telephone conversations beginning 'I told you not to ring me here'.)

There is also a fair amount of ogling, bottom-patting and lewd comment, considered by men to be part of their civil liberties, until defined as sexual harassment. A key aspect of successful bluffing is never to get too serious, so should this topic arise we recommend a quick escape via a comment to the effect that men find it difficult to differentiate between friendly banter which acknowledges gender-differences and a bit of harmless flirting on the one hand, and what is deemed offensive behaviour on the other. As in all things, they can be guaranteed to overstep the mark on occasions, if not regularly.

Men feel they have made great strides in owning that new rules apply. It cannot be helped if some of them harbour resentment that certain successful women in work and business exploit their femininity to ruthless effect. It does, however, mean that men, too, can now be accused of sleeping their way to the top.

## Shopping

You can safely assert that the majority of men dislike shopping. It not only means spending money, but making snap decisions. They like armchair shopping first, studying advertisements, comparing prices before going out to buy a car, a house, farmland, a factory, a company or an international corporation. The purchase of a lettuce, cat food or air freshener does not excite them.

A man will be happy for a while in a hardware shop if he badly needs a hammer or 200 yards of plastic tubing. But shopping, in general, seems to him to be a waste of time. A mega waste of time as far as he is concerned, is window shopping. This he does not understand at all. The joy of staring at goods for sale which cannot be bought because the shop is closed is quite beyond his comprehension.

## Dress sense

Young men might choose to buy collarless shirts, crocodile shoes and Dennis-the-Menace socks, but once into their middle age, men rarely buy any clothes at all. There is a marketing secret with which you can amuse people should talk turn to this subject: advertisements for male underwear are placed in locations where women will see them, not because this turns women on (which is what men like to think), but because it is the women who buy them. It's a tradition that starts with their mothers, is taken up by their girlfriends and ends with their wives.

Alternatively, you might demonstrate the 'men are disinterested in clothes' thesis by asking one of your male bluffees when he last bought himself a pair of underpants. He is quite likely to avoid the question. Wait for him to refer to the fabulous set of silky underclothes he bought for his girlfriend or wife – skimpy, lacy, revealing, with suspenders. Then reply: "Just what she always wanted." But take care to inject the comment with sufficient humour. Causing members of the audience to walk away never reflects well on a bluffer.

Most men will vacuum the entire house or start concreting the drive rather than go to a clothes shop. They will adopt a set of tatty clothes in which they feel most comfortable for all the hours outside work – a favourite woolly jumper, frayed jeans or kneed cords and a T-shirt advertising some nostalgic memory of misspent youth. Making them part with them is like separating a baby from its comforter.

Similarly, many men appear welded, as well as wedded, to their socks – despite clear evidence that wandering round the bedroom dressed only in stretch nylon (sizes 8 to 11) makes them look about as sexy as suet pudding. This is not some form of perversion, it's linear thinking. Socks are the last item of clothing to be removed. They remain on the top of the heap of clothes overnight, and so are the first to be put on in the morning. And men are nothing if not creatures of habit.

Many men are frightened of looking sexy, feeling that this is the province of women, and that there is something essentially female about being concerned with one's looks at all. What does it matter to a man if the elastic has gone in his Y fronts? What's wrong with underpants so old that they have taken on the colour of storm cloud and the texture of wire wool? Minimalist designs and silky fabrics are for lingerie freaks, not for real men. Offer the thought that were men to wear something soft next to their skin, the next you know they'd be behaving like women: waxing their legs, changing their minds, and gossiping.

## Shaving

Men shave because it's a macho occupation. They love the terrifying scrape of cold steel across the face, the delicate work round the lips, the surgical precision needed at the entrances to the nostrils, the scars so bravely borne when things go wrong. It's the nearest they get to the duelling clubs of Old Heidelberg. Besides which, shaving is the one skill men possess that nobody has taught them.

Shaving is a ritual that shapes the day. Men's facial hair grows at the rate of about 12 inches a year, and it takes on average about two and a half days each year to keep it under control. So it gives a man ample opportunity to admire himself regularly in the mirror without arousing the least suspicion that he is vain.

Young men seem unsure at present whether to shave or not – designer stubble attracts young women but alienates their mothers. Men who grow beards are thought by many to be hiding a sense of inferiority, which they frequently are. But before the invention of breakfast cereals, which are known to have a magnetic attraction to beards, men made full cosmetic use of facial hair, sporting extravagant sideboards, handlebar moustaches, pencil moustaches, goatees and beards like lion's manes. Untrimmed beards could reach enormous proportions – the longest recorded was over 17 feet. Today, if men don't shave, their wives may complain of the bristles. They may also compare them to a lavatory brush, and tell them to stand upside down next to the loo to make themselves useful.

## Sport

It is generally believed that men play sports for their health. This is only partly true. Most take exercise as a kind of balancing act. They heave and sweat around the rugby pitch in order to make space for the quantity of beer they will later consume.

Sport serves two useful functions for men, apart from keeping fit:

1  It tires them out.
2  It gives them something to talk about. Most young men develop an interest in sport because it is a way of communicating with their fathers.

Three out of four men take part in some form of sport every week, while just over half of women feel the need. Women play sports to lose weight and participate; men play sports to win. Even when they are pounding the footpaths in a late-night jog they are secretly pounding the table at a conference, flooring their rivals with their sharpened acumen.

Sport also provides the best excuse for unbridled behaviour, such as spitting, shouting, swearing, scratching the testicles, and flattening others – and all that while watching television.

# TOUCHY SUBJECTS

## Giving up seats

There was a time when men would open doors for women, and unhesitatingly offer their seat on public transport. During the great years of strident feminism such behaviour might have been rewarded with a stern lecture. Men learnt to get on a bus or a train without looking sideways, and instantly bury their heads in a newspaper.

Yet many men still feel an atavistic urge to give way to women. They are not actually reading those papers, but staring blankly at the print while they assess whether the woman standing over them is pregnant or decrepit enough to justify rising. These are the men who have all made critical mistakes in the past – the grey-haired female who did not appreciate being labelled as old and frail; the woman with a weight problem who did not realise it was quite that bad. Some men in the throes of this dilemma will never come to anyone's notice – they don't dare sit down at all.

## Seeking advice

Men like to sort out their own problems. Only if they cannot do so will they reluctantly seek the advice and help of others. It puts them in an awkward position: it makes them look weak and vulnerable.

Neither men nor women, but particularly women, should volunteer advice to a man, especially about a manly task. A delightful trick to play when discussing this topic is to adopt a sombre demeanour, then offer your listeners the following tip: if any of them – and God forbid they should – ever find themselves in the position of having to give a man advice (in order, for instance, to prevent a disaster), they must – must – disguise it as support, and preferably try to make it look as if it was his idea in the first place.

## Being single

Being a bachelor has little of the stigma attached to being 'an old maid'. Once over a certain age, a single male becomes eligible for the epithet 'confirmed bachelor', a term which is now open to interpretation of the nudge-nudge, wink-wink kind. This is about the one aspect of single men's lives that does not turn married men green with envy. That, and their shorter life expectancy (by some 5 years) than married ones.

Single men are highly sensitive to the fact that the rest of the world is couple-oriented. Their friends are constantly trying to marry them off, as if trying to ensure that everyone is infected with the same virus – a sort of societal inoculation against envy of the single state.

## Height

The ideal man projected by films, advertising and classical myths is athletic and tall – qualities that by extension are also associated with virtues such as courage, loyalty, honesty, and an immediate advantage in the basketball team. Height seems to express authority. In the 20th century, 80% of U.S. presidential elections were won by the taller candidate.

Short men are very conscious of their standing. It is often suggested that they compensate by exaggerated behaviour that gets them noticed, by becoming tyrannical, witty or enormously rich. But nothing compensates for the uncomfortable fact that they have to look up to the other men and, worse still, look up to many women. Women offer little consolation: most say that they would prefer a man taller than themselves as a partner. In only one marriage in 720 is the woman taller than the man, and veteran film star Mickey Rooney (5 ft 1 ins – 1.55 m), married eight times, accounts for more than his fair share of them.

Short men will rarely admit that they are short, or want to talk about it. If the conversation is unavoidable, you might like to list some famous men who are, or were, vertically challenged: Wayne Sleep is 5 ft 2 ins (1.57 m); Humphrey Bogart was 5 ft 4 ins (1.62 m). Tom Cruise is 5 ft 5 1/2 ins (1.66 m), Al Pacino is 5 ft 6 ins (1.67 m), as was Frank Sinatra; John Lennon was 5 ft 7 ins (1.70 m) and so is Sylvester Stallone and Mick Jagger; though these statistics should be given maximum headroom since no celebrity is likely to submit to being measured against a doorjamb.

## Shape

Men are conscious of their bodies. They have seen women swoon over the rippling biceps and washboard stomachs of the superstars. But it is a hard task for most men to achieve this kind of physique without immense effort, and they soon suspect that they do not need to bother.

One in three men believe that they are overweight and are worried about the shape of their stomach. Yet after the age of 40, many men secretly accept that they will never see their feet again. 'Take me as I am,' they declare, and many woman do.

## Castration

This is one to avoid. Most men will deny that they have a castration complex, which may simply encourage you to feel that Sigmund Freud was probably right to suggest that they did.

Not that this ground is entirely barren from a bluffer's point of view. Raise the subject of Lorena Bobbit, who in 1993 severed her husband's penis with a kitchen knife. Then remind everyone that she was acquitted, and enjoy watching all the men squirm. This will do very little for your status as an expert, but at least it will give you a laugh. Why should your bluffees have all the fun?

## Circumcision

Sanitary considerations seem to be at the root of male circumcision. It has been practised among the ancient Egyptians, the Incas of Peru, all Muslims, all Jews, many African tribes and the Australian aborigines. What they all have in common is the desert, and everyone knows how pernicious sand is.

These days men do not so frequently come with this option. In the U.K. fewer than 10% of boys are now circumcised. But they remain concerned about which model women prefer – Roundheads or Cavaliers.

Many women seem uneasy about the idea of such muti-lation, though they may express a preference for its aesthetic effects. It is principally circumcised men who are used in nude photographs. Women also attest that the Roundhead is a better stayer because it has been exposed to years of inside-trouser friction. Mention that around a dinner table and you will soon divine who is which.

## That time of the month

Men cannot bear talking about menstruation. They don't even like to think about it. In Bali, menstruating women are exiled to huts outside the village compound because they are held to be vulnerable to evil spirits. To many men that seems just about right: menstruation represents the direct opposite to everything a woman is supposed to be.

The very idea of it makes men blush. There is only one thing worse: when men try to talk about it frankly and honestly. Then women blush.

## Snoring

This is a hardy perennial for those bluffing about men, due to its near-perfect combination of ubiquity and comic value. Be prepared for men to go on the defensive; most of them spend their lives being criticised for snoring. Keep them on your side by revealing that women snore as well. It's just that women are the lighter sleepers, so wake up more often to the vibrating sounds in their partner's soft palate and so-called 'posterior faucal pillars'.

Snoring occurs when lying face up, so various precautions can be taken. A sheet of sandpaper can be sewn into the back of the pyjama top, for example, or a hairbrush can be placed in the trousers. Whistling in the snorer's ear often changes the sleep pattern and stops the snoring. Other than that, it's best if he sleeps in another room.

## Hypochondria

It is widely held that women can bear more pain than men – that men could not tolerate the excruciating pain of childbirth. This proposition will be triumphantly shot down by men using the argument that it can never be put to the test.

Meanwhile, men make a great play of putting up with

ailments. They will happily go to work with a thick cold, sneeze and cough all day, infect everyone else in the effort to convince them that they are martyrs to their work, then take the next two weeks off.

Lurking behind their bravado, however, is a strange contradiction. When men are ill, it is never with anything trivial. A sore throat could be laryngitis, a touch of indigestion may be the onset of renal failure, tiredness is exhaustion, pins and needles may presage cardiac arrest, a spot could well be skin cancer. They convince themselves they may be going to die.

This fear will not lead them to the doctor. They don't want to hear they are going to die. Neither do they want to be told that they have nothing more than a minor indisposition. They would rather die.

In fact, not going to the doctor means that men run the risk of contracting long-term illnesses that could have been diagnosed earlier. It may also account to some extent for the fact that men have a shorter average life expectancy than women, by five years – 74 as opposed to 79.

But men, being silent martyrs to their ailments, are most intolerant of women who complain legitimately of theirs. 'Yes, I had that last week,' they will assert, and this sentence continues in a think-bubble over their head, 'and I didn't make that kind of fuss.' Women's illnesses are inconvenient, exaggerated and, worst of all, could upstage their own.

## Grey hair

It is said that men with grey hair, or greying temples, look more distinguished, more attractive and more intelligent than those without. This is of course a myth put out by clever wives and girlfriends.

The astute grey-haired man will douse his scalp

liberally with a product which turns his hair to a shade of mid-mouse, knowing that it takes years off his age. It may – possibly – be worth reminding people that they should never draw attention to discernable tints in a man's hair. But on no account should you say that it will lead to 'hairy moments'. Nothing diminishes a bluffer's standing more than a feeble joke.

## No hair

Men need some comfort about hair loss. It is best if they go bald when they are about 23, when they still believe they have other things going for them. At 45 they need consolation; denial is something they can do for themselves.

The Japanese have always associated baldness with high levels of sexual activity. In fact, they are thinking of excessive sexual activity and reprehensible dissipation, which is deemed both damaging and ridiculous, but you do not have to mention this. Nor the fact that in some parts of the Far East, baldness is so rare that when people come across it, they just fall about laughing.

Men think that hair – real or false – is a sine qua non of sex appeal, and no amount of reasoning will tell them otherwise. Women consistently say that baldness doesn't matter; that bald men are attractive; that, after all, they adore babies and most of them are bald. But if cornered by a man insisting that truly, honestly, he really does not mind a pristine pate – you should offer reassurance by quoting some scientific evidence for the idea that bald men are sexier. It has been shown that testosterone directly affects hair growth by starving hair roots in the scalp in order to apply itself elsewhere.

A new treatment for baldness which encourages hair growth contains an agent prohibiting the production of dihydrotestosterone. The trouble is that this results in a loss of sex drive, which is somewhat counterproductive.

Should you by any chance find yourself conversing on this topic with a follicly-challenged man who has, for whatever reason, lost your sympathy, you could amuse yourself by telling him that there is one guaranteed method of restoring up to 40% of hair loss. Wait for his eager cry of 'Oh really, what's that?' Then inform him that it's castration.

But it's a bit of an extreme measure.

## THINGS MEN DO THAT ANNOY WOMEN

Asking where something is before starting to look for it.

Hovering at the door, calling out the time; then, when she's ready, remembering something you have to do that will delay the getaway.

Not listening with the appropriate amount of interest.

Giving her a wheelbarrow for Christmas because it's something you want.

Being reluctant to accept invitations to go out; once out, being difficult to get back home again.

Saying: 'I didn't buy you chocolates because I thought you would say you were on a diet.'

Buying the right garment in the right colour but the wrong size.

Telling her that *'We've* run out of toothpaste/peanut butter/ batteries/beer…'

Failing to notice that she has changed her hair/ revamped her wardrobe/lost weight.

Getting on better with her mother than she does herself.

Leaving stubble in the basin.

Putting a fortnight's unsorted washing into the machine and turning everything pink.

Blaming the dog.


## WOMEN'S APHORISMS ABOUT MEN

Dogs are more rewarding than men because:

You can house train a dog.

Dogs at least make an attempt at finding what they've mislaid before appealing to you.

Middle-aged dogs don't feel the need to abandon you for a younger owner.

\* \* \* \*

Men are like mascara. They usually run at the first sign of emotion.

The best way to get a man to do something is to suggest that he is too old for it.

55

A man having a sense of humour does not mean that he laughs at your jokes. It means you laugh at his.

A man marries a woman expecting that she won't change, but she does. A woman marries a man expecting that he will change, but he doesn't.

Men seldom make passes at a girl who surpasses.

A man's got to do what a man's got to do. A woman must do what he won't.

\* \* \* \*

Men are like computers because:

In order to get their attention, you have to turn them on.

Big power surges knock them out for the rest of the night.

## GLOSSARY

**Andropause** The male menopause. The jury is still out on whether this is a valid concept; some call it 'getting old'.

**Bachelor** Man who gets tangled up with a number of women in order to avoid getting tied up with one.

**Condom** Contraceptive device which doubles as a brake.

**Family crown jewels** Reproductive organs; also referred to as equipment, wedding tackle, meat and two veg, the dangly bits, and the full Monty.

**Friend** Someone to whom a man can admit sexual disaster, having already failed to buy his round.

**Fwaw!** Expression of appreciation of female sexual desirability by one who has already decided that he has no hope of fulfilling it.

**Gentleman** One who takes the weight on his knees and elbows.

**Husband** A man who has given himself the opportunity of committing another sin, adultery.

**Impotence** Spending all night trying to do once what you once spent all night doing.

**Man's man** One who exemplifies what men want to find in men.

**Mate** Not the woman a man is sleeping with, but the chap who shares a six-pack with him when his team has won the Cup.

**Men** Boys who have finished growing.

**Misogynist** Hater of women. No known inverse. An ancient Greek word; Plato thought women should be classed with children and slaves.

**Nymphomaniac** A woman who appreciates sex in almost the same quantity and breadth as men.

**Penis** The male organ, also known as Bishop, chopper, cock, dick, dong, John Thomas, knob, one-eyed trouser snake, pecker, percy, plonker, pork sword, prick, prong, skyscraper, tail, tassel, todger, tool, wick, widger, willy, winkie, whirley-wha (Scots).

**Polygamy** One man, many wives; a male fantasy, until he works out the cost.

**Rat** A rival, a.k.a. cad, bounder, knave, rotter, two-timing bastard.

**Testicles** Sperm manufacturing units; a.k.a. balls, bollocks, cojones, gonads, goolies, pocket billiards, testes, knackers and nuts.

**Testosterone** The male hormone which gives men their virile qualities, their sex drive, and their smell.

**Wanker** A man who masturbates; hence, effectively, any man.

**Wet dream** Nocturnal emissions. The male sex drive's way of saying who is boss.

**Wife** A woman who sticks with her husband through all the troubles he wouldn't have had if he hadn't married her.

**Womaniser** One who has the success with women that all men envy, a.k.a. rake, philanderer, wolf, stud, lucky swine.

**WHT** Wandering hand trouble, a feature of the inept womaniser, and the dirty old man.

# THE AUTHOR

Antony Mason is the author of some 40 books on travel, exploration, history, geography, spying, volleyball, house plants, the Belgians… In other words, he is a consummate bluffer, though he would not put it like that, publicly at least.

Like most males, as a boy he was constantly urged to be a man. Now that he is one, he realises that this is one of the world's greatest bluffs. Although well into his forties, if separated from a mirror he imagines he is about 18, and certainly wishes he was – were it possible to do without all those sticky agonies of adolescence.

'In your dreams,' interjects his wife. 'Forty-something going on fourteen,' she would say. But then women think they know all about men – a prejudice that the author would like to shoot down with all guns blazing. Neeeeorrrrrr! Dat-dat-dat-dat-dat-dat!

# THE CONTRIBUTORS

Acknowledgement and thanks are given to Drew Launay and Nick Yapp for their contributions to this guide, and to the unknown originators of the points on pages 55/56.

# the Bluffer's® Guides

The five million copy best-selling
humour series that contains facts,
jargon and inside information –
all you need to know to hold your
own among experts.

---

Accountancy

Astrology &
    Fortune Telling

Archaeology

Bond

The Classics

Chess

Computers

Consultancy

The Cosmos

Cricket

Divorce

Doctors

Economics

The Flight Deck

Football

Genetics

Golf

Jazz

Law

Management

Marketing

Men

Men & Women

Middle Age

Music

Opera

Philosophy

Psychology

Public Speaking

The Quantum
    Universe

Relationships

Rugby

Seduction

Sex

Skiing

Small Business

Stocks & Shares

Tax

Teaching

University

Whisky

Wine

Women

---

Available from all good bookshops, online, or direct from the
publisher: in the U.K. (0)207 582 7123 (post free), and in the
U.S.A. 1-800-243-0495 (toll free). **www.bluffers.com**